Festivals through the Year
Winter

Anita Ganeri

Heinemann
LIBRARY

First published in Great Britain by Heinemann Library
Halley Court, Jordan Hill, Oxford OX2 8EJ
a division of Reed Educational and Professional Publishing Ltd.
Heinemann is a registered trademark of Reed Educational & Professional Publishing Limited.

OXFORD MELBOURNE AUCKLAND IBADAN JOHANNESBURG
BLANTYRE GABORONE PORTSMOUTH (NH) USA CHICAGO

Designed by Ken Vail Graphic Design, Cambridge
Illustrations by Pat Murray
Printed in China

05
10 9 8 7 6 5 4 3

ISBN 0 431 05464 9
This title is also available in a library hardback edition (ISBN 0 431 05459 2)

British Library Cataloguing in Publication Data

Ganeri, Anita
Winter. – (Festivals through the year)
1. Winter festivals – Great Britain – Juvenile literature
I. Title
394.2'61'0941

Acknowledgements
The Publishers would like to thank the following for permission to reproduce photographs:
Andes Press Agency/Carlos Reyes Manzo, pp. 9, 11, 19, 24; Collections, (Geoff Howard) pp. 14, 17, 29, (Brian Shuel) pp. 13, 22, 26, 28; Emmet, Phil & Val, pp. 12, 25; FLPA/Hamblin, A.R., p. 23; J. Allan Cash, p.4; Sanders, Peter, pp. 8, 10; Soester, Juliette, p. 6; Still Moving, (Andrea Cringean) p. 20, (Angus Johnston) p.21.

Cover photograph reproduced with permission of Collections/Brian Shuel

Our thanks to Peter Woodward, who works with SHAP Working Party on World Religions in Education, for his comments in the preparation of this book.

Every effort has been made to contact copyright holders of any material reproduced in this book. Any omissions will be rectified in subsequent printings if notice is given to the Publisher

Contents

Celebrating winter 4

Hanukkah 6

Ramadan 8

Laylat-ul-Qadr 10

Id-ul-Fitr 11

Advent Sunday 12

Christmas 13

New Year 16

Epiphany 18

Guru Gobind Singh's birthday 19

Burn's Night 20

St Valentine's Day 22

Mahashivratri 24

Shrove Tuesday 26

Chinese New Year 28

Glossary 30

Index 32

Words printed in **bold letters like these** are explained in the Glossary.

Celebrating winter

Winter is a time for keeping warm. The days are short, dark and cold. All around, nature lies bare and barren. The trees lose their leaves and the plants die down. The ground is dusted with frost or snow. In the past, the start of winter was a busy time as people prepared their stores of food to last them until the spring.

Many festivals are held in winter. Some celebrate the beginning of the New Year. Others have special religious meanings, when people remember the lives of their gods and teachers and important times in their religion's history.

A snowy winter's day.

Festivals are often happy times with many ways of celebrating. There are special services and ceremonies, delicious food, dancing, cards and gifts. Some festivals are holidays when you have a day off school.

Some festivals happen on the same day each year. Others change from year to year. For festivals that change, you will find a dates circle, which tells you when the festival will be. (The future dates of some festivals are only decided upon nearer the time, so some dates in the circles may be out by a day or two.)

Dates

7 January 1998
26 January 1999
15 January 2000
4 January 2001
9 January 2002

Moon dates

The calendar we use every day has a year of 365 days, divided into 12 months. Most months have 30 or 31 days. Some religions use different calendars which are based on the Moon. A Moon month is the time it takes for the Moon to travel around the Earth. This is about 27 days, which gives a shorter year. So, each year, the Moon calendar falls out of step with the everyday calendar. This is why some festivals fall on different days each year.

Hanukkah

The **Jewish** festival of Hanukkah happens in December. It reminds **Jews** of a time, long ago, when a wicked king ruled over them. He marched into **Jerusalem** and ransacked the Temple, the Jews' holiest place. After two years of fighting, the Jews won back their city. They tried to light the **Menorah**, the special lamp in the Temple. But there was only enough oil for one day. The Jews prayed to God and a **miracle** happened. God kept the lamp burning for eight days until they fetched more oil. That is why Hanukkah lasts for eight days.

Playing dreidle

Dreidle is a special game played at Hanukkah. The dreidle is a spinning top with four sides. Each side has a letter from the Jewish alphabet. These are the first letters of the words 'A great miracle happened here'. Each letter is also an instruction. It tells the player to take a sweet from the pile or to give a sweet back.

Jews celebrate Hanukkah by lighting a nine-branched menorah, or candlestick. They light one candle on the first night, two on the second night, and so on. The ninth candle is used to light the others. There are also parties and presents for children.

Dates

14 December 1998
4 December 1999
22 December 2000
10 December 2001
30 November 2002

Lighting the Hanukkah candles.

Ramadan

Every year, during the month of Ramadan, **Muslims fast** from dawn to sunset. This means that they have nothing to eat or drink. Muslims fast because **Allah** tells them to do so in the Qur'an, their **holy** book. They believe that fasting shows that they are living as Allah wishes them to. It also reminds them of poor and hungry people.

Dates

19 December 1998
9 December 1999
27 November 2000
17 November 2001
6 November 2002

A family breaks their fast with water and dates at the end of a Ramadan day.

Some people do not have to fast. Pregnant women and people who are ill or on a journey are excused. They make up for it by fasting later on or giving money to the poor. Young children do not have to fast.

During Ramadan, Muslims eat breakfast before **dawn**. Then they fast until sunset when they have a light snack before evening prayers. After prayers, they eat their main meal of the day.

Muslims praying in a **mosque**.

Five Pillars

*Fasting during Ramadan is one of the Five Pillars of **Islam**. These are five duties Muslims try to carry out:*

1 *Believing in Allah and in **Prophet Muhammad (pbuh)**.*
2 *Praying five times a day.*
3 *Giving money to the poor.*
4 *Fasting during Ramadan.*
5 *Making the **Hajj pilgrimage** to **Makkah**.*

Laylat-ul-Qadr

Dates

24 January 1998
14 January 1999
3 January 2000
11 December 2001
1 December 2002

On the 27th day of Ramadan, **Muslims** celebrate the festival of Laylat-ul-Qadr. Its name means the Night of Power. It remembers the night on which the **Angel Jibril** gave the first part of the Qur'an to the **Prophet Muhammad (pbuh)**. The Qur'an is the Muslims' **holy** book. Muslims believe that it contains the exact words of **Allah**. Through the Angel Jibril, Allah gave the Qur'an to Muhammad who taught it to his followers. To mark this special time, many Muslims stay up all night, praying and reading the Qur'an.

Reading the Qur'an.

The Qur'an

Muslims learn verses from the Qur'an and use them in their prayers. The Qur'an tells them how Allah wants them to live and worship.

Id-ul-Fitr

Dates

29 January 1998
19 January 1999
8 January 2000
17 December 2001
6 December 2002

The **Muslim** festival of Id-ul-Fitr comes at the end of Ramadan. This marks the end of **fasting** and is a very happy time. It begins when the New Moon appears in the sky and lasts for three days. Before Id starts, Muslims give money to the poor. This is one of the Five Pillars of **Islam** (see page 9). Then they visit the **mosque** to say special Id prayers which thank **Allah** for making them strong enough to fast. Afterwards, they celebrate with parties and presents for their friends and family.

Many Muslims send each other cards to wish each other 'Id Mubarak', or Happy Id. (Id is also spelt Eid.)

Advent Sunday

The fourth Sunday before Christmas is called Advent Sunday. Advent means 'coming'. This is the time when **Christians** look forward to Christmas when they celebrate **Jesus**'s birthday. On Advent Sunday, Christians go to a special service in **church**. They also light the first candle in an Advent crown. This is a circle of holly with four small candles, one for each Sunday of Advent. A larger candle often stands in the middle. It is lit on Christmas Day.

Dates

29 November 1998
28 November 1999
3 December 2000
2 December 2001
1 December 2002

An Advent crown.

Advent calendar

Some people use a special Advent calendar to mark off the days up to Christmas. Each day, you open a window. Inside there is usually a Christmas picture, such as an angel or a shining star.

Christmas

Every year, on 25 December, **Christians** remember **Jesus**'s birthday. This is called Christmas Day. Jesus is very important for Christians. They believe that he was the son of God. No one knows exactly when Jesus was born. The first Christians chose 25 December as his birthday because it was the date of another ancient winter festival.

The story of Jesus's birth is told in the Bible, the Christians' **holy** book. Jesus was born in a stable in **Bethlehem**. His mother was called Mary. When they heard the news that a special baby had been born, shepherds and **Wise Men** came to visit him and bring him gifts. At Christmas, children often act out the Christmas story at school. This is called a **nativity** play.

Putting on a nativity play.

Christmas (2)

Opening your Christmas presents is very exciting!

Christmas is a very happy time. Many **Christians** go to **church** to thank God for sending **Jesus** to them. They listen to readings from the Bible, say prayers and sing Christmas songs, called **carols**. Afterwards, they eat a special meal and give each other presents. These remind them of the gifts given to Jesus. They are often placed around a Christmas tree, which is beautifully decorated with tinsel and lights.

The day after Christmas Day is called Boxing Day. Many years ago, people put money and clothes in boxes for the poor. The boxes were opened and shared out on Boxing Day.

Santa Claus

According to legend, the first Santa Claus, or Father Christmas, was St Nicholas, the **patron saint** of children. He was a kind man who gave children presents to reward them for being good. Santa Claus still brings presents on Christmas **Eve**. But only if you are fast asleep!

New Year

1 January is New Year's Day. This is a time for looking forward and wishing for a good year ahead. It is also a holiday.

People welcome in the New Year on the night before. This is called New Year's **Eve**. In Scotland, people celebrate with a lively festival called Hogmanay. There are parties, fireworks, singing and dancing, to ring out the old year and ring in the new. As the clock strikes midnight, people link arms and sing a song called Auld Lang Syne. It reminds them of old and new friends.

Singing Auld Lang Syne at Hogmanay.

There are many **customs** linked to New Year. One is called first-footing. If the first person to come to your house after midnight is a tall, dark-haired man, you will have good luck in the

Welcoming the New Year in London.

coming year. The first-footer should bring a lump of coal as a gift. This is a way of wishing warmth and happiness to your household.

1 January 2000 is a very special New Year's Day. This is the first day of a new millennium. A millennium lasts for 1000 years.

Making resolutions

The New Year is a time for a fresh start and for making New Year's resolutions. These are a bit like promises. For example, you might promise to keep your room tidy. How long can you keep your resolutions for?

17

Epiphany

Epiphany falls on 6 January. This is when **Christians** celebrate the visit of the three **Wise Men** to the baby **Jesus**. Some Christians also remember two later events in Jesus's life. One is his **baptism**. The other is the first **miracle** Jesus performed.

Epiphany is the twelfth, and last, day of Christmas. You should take down your Christmas cards and decorations and pack them away until next year. It is unlucky to leave them up any longer.

Three wise children!

King Bean and Queen Pea

In some places, a special cake was baked for Twelfth Night with a dried pea and bean hidden inside it. If you got one of these, you were King Bean or Queen Pea for the last day of Christmas fun.

Guru Gobind Singh's birthday

On 5 January each year, **Sikhs** remember the birthday of **Guru Gobind Singh** who was born in 1675. He was the last of the ten Sikh **Gurus**, or teachers. He began the **Khalsa**, a group of Sikhs who have become full members of their faith. Before he died, Guru Gobind Singh did not choose a person to be the next Guru. Instead he named the Sikhs' **holy** book, the Guru Granth Sahib, as their teacher.

Sikhs celebrate this special day with a festival called a **Gurpurb**. In the **Gurdwara**, the Guru Granth Sahib is read right through from beginning to end. People sing **hymns** in the Guru's memory and share a meal. There is also a procession through the streets.

Guru Gobind Singh.

Burn's Night

On 25 January, Scottish people mark the birthday of Robert Burns, Scotland's most famous poet. He was born in 1759. On Burn's Night, they hold a special feast to celebrate his life and work. Many people dress in **tartan** for the evening.

The highlight of the Burn's Night feast is a special Scottish dish, called haggis. This is like a pudding, made of minced meat, oatmeal and spices. It is brought to the table on a huge plate, as a piper plays the **bagpipes** and all the guests slowly clap their hands. Then one of the guests **recites** a poem which Burns wrote in the haggis's honour!

The haggis is cut. It will be eaten with mashed neeps (swede) and tatties (potatoes).

After the dinner, there are lots of speeches. Some guests stand up and recite more of Burns's poems. Then the singing and dancing begin. Everyone has a very jolly time.

Robert Burns's statue in Edinburgh.

A Red, Red Rose

Here are a few lines from one of Robert Burn's most famous poems. Perhaps you could learn it for the next Burn's Night?

'O, my Luve's like a red, red rose
That's newly sprung in June.
O, my Luve's like the melodie
That's sweetly play'd in tune.'

St Valentine's Day

St Valentine's Day falls on 14 February. This is a time for sending cards or flowers to someone you love. Traditionally, the cards are meant to come from secret admirers. So people change their handwriting or just put a question mark inside to hide their true **identity**!

St Valentine's Day gets its name from two **saints** who lived hundreds of years ago. Both were **holy** men who were killed for their beliefs. Legend says that one of them wrote a last message to the lady he loved on the wall of his prison cell. He signed it from 'Your Valentine'.

Toys and cards for Valentine's Day.

Another story says that St Valentine's Day was the day when birds chose their mates and began to build their nests. This marked the very beginning of spring.

Birds find their mates in the spring.

In some places, St Valentine's Day was the time when young men and women began to think about getting married. For fun, they played a game to help them find a wife or husband. Everyone's name was written on a scrap of paper. Then each boy picked a girl's name and each girl picked a boy's name.

Be my Valentine

Try making your own Valentine's card. Decorate it with hearts or red roses and write a verse inside. Don't forget to disguise your handwriting so the other person does not guess who it is from.

23

Mahashivratri

The **Hindu** festival of Mahashivratri happens in February or March, on the night of the Full Moon. This is a special night when people worship the great god, **Shiva.**

Shiva is a very important Hindu god. He destroys evil in the world. He is said to live on a high mountain in the **Himalayas** with his wife, Parvati, a beautiful goddess. They have two sons, Ganesha, the elephant god, and six-headed Skanda. Shiva rides on a huge white bull, called Nandi.

Shiva and Parvati in a Hindu **mandir**.

Dates

25 February 1998
15 February 1999
4 March 2000
21 February 2001

Later dates not known

Breaking the fast
with festival food
in a mandir.

During the festival, many Hindus **fast**.
This means they have nothing to eat or
drink. Some spend the whole night in the
mandir. They say prayers, sing songs of
worship and tell stories about Shiva.
They also make offerings of flowers and
milk. Next morning, they go home, have
a bath and break their fast with a meal.

Shiva and the holy river

This story tells how the **River Ganges** fell from
heaven to Earth. Shiva caught it in his long hair
to break its fall. Then he let it flow gently across
the land. Otherwise, its great weight would have
crushed the Earth.

Shrove Tuesday

Shrove Tuesday is the day before Lent. This is the name for the six weeks before **Easter**. Lent is a very special, solemn time for **Christians**. They remember the days **Jesus** spent in the desert, thinking about how to do God's work. At Lent, Christians try to live good lives and to think about Jesus's suffering. Many people give up something they enjoy, like eating sweets.

Shrove Tuesday is also called Pancake Day. People used to eat very plain foods during Lent. So, on Shrove Tuesday, they used up any rich foods left in the house, like eggs and oil. These were made into delicious, sizzling pancakes. Today, people still mark Shrove Tuesday by making pancakes and even holding pancake races.

Who will win the pancake race?

Making pancakes

Ask an adult to help you.
This amount makes eight pancakes.

You will need:
225g plain flour
pinch of salt
1 egg
275ml milk
oil

What to do:
1 Put the flour and salt in a large bowl,
   add the egg and mix well.
2 Beat in the milk until the mixture
   is smooth.
3 Stir in 1 teaspoonful of oil and leave
   to stand for 30 minutes.
4 Heat a pan and add a few drops of oil.
5 Pour in some batter and swirl it around
   to cover the pan.
6 Cook for about 2 minutes, then turn
   the pancake and cook the other side
   for 1 minute. Add sugar and lemon
   juice, and eat!

Chinese New Year

In January or February, Chinese people welcome in the new year with a very colourful festival. People decorate their homes and streets with strings of lanterns. They also let off firecrackers to scare off evil **spirits**. The highlight of the festival is the famous lion dance. Two dancers, dressed in a lion costume, dance through the streets. People give the lion money and food to bring good luck.

Many delicious types of food are enjoyed at Chinese New Year. Each one has a special meaning. Noodles are eaten for a long life. Green vegetables are signs of the coming of spring. Red or pink-coloured food, such as prawns, brings happiness and luck.

Give the lion some money if you want to have good luck!

Dates

28 January 1998 (Tiger)
16 February 1999 (Hare)
5 February 2000 (Dragon)
24 January 2001 (Snake)
12 February 2002 (Horse)

Happy New Year!

Each Chinese New Year is named after an animal. Legend says that the **Buddha** once called all the animals together. But only 12 came. They were the Rat, Ox, Tiger, Hare, Dragon, Snake, Horse, Goat, Monkey, Rooster, Dog and Pig. As a reward, the Buddha gave each of them a year to look after. Can you find out which year you were born in?

Red for luck

To celebrate the New Year, children are given gifts of lucky money, wrapped in red or gold paper envelopes. Red and gold are believed to be lucky colours, bringing health, wealth and wisdom.

Glossary

Allah – Muslim word for God

Angel Jibril – angel sent by Allah to teach Muhammad (pbuh) the word of the Qur'an

bagpipes – musical instrument, often played in Scotland

baptism – ceremony held when a person becomes a full member of the Christian Church. It marked the start of Jesus's teaching.

Bethlehem – town in Israel where Jesus was born

Buddha – great teacher who lived in India about 2500 years ago

carol – special song sung at Christmas

Christian – person who follows the teachings of Jesus

church – Christian place of worship

custom – special way of doing things, such as celebrating a festival

dawn – early in the morning, when the Sun rises

Easter – spring festival at which Christians remember how Jesus died and how he came back to life again

eve – the night before. Christmas Eve is the night before Christmas.

fast – to go without anything to eat or drink

Gurdwara – Sikh place of worship

Gurpurb – Sikh festival which celebrates the birth or death of one of the Gurus

Guru Gobind Singh – Sikh leader who started the Khalsa

Guru – Sikh teacher or leader

Hajj – pilgrimage made by Muslims to Makkah

Himalayas – series of mountain ranges curving from Pakistan in the west to Tibet in the east

Hindu – to do with the Hindu religion, which began in India about 4500 years ago. A Hindu is someone who follows the Hindu religion.

holy – means respected because it is to do with God

hymn – song of worship

identity – your identity means who you are

Islam – religion of the Muslims. It began about 1400 years ago in Saudi Arabia.

Jerusalem – city in Israel which is very important for Jews, Christians and Muslims

Jesus – religious teacher who lived about 2000 years ago. Christians believe that he was the son of God.

Jewish – to do with the Jewish religion

Jew – person who follows the Jewish religion, which began in the Middle East more than 4000 years ago

Khalsa – Sikh community, or family. A special ceremony is held for Sikhs joining the Khalsa.

Makkah – city in the country we now called Saudi Arabia where the Prophet Muhammad was born. It is the Muslims' holiest place.

mandir – Hindu place of worship, also called a temple

Menorah – candlestick with seven or nine branches from the first Jewish temple. Copies are now used in Jewish ceremonies and festivals.

miracle – an amazing event

mosque – Muslim place of worship

Muhammad – the last great prophet of Islam. He was chosen by Allah to teach people how to live.

Muslim – follower of the religion of Islam

nativity – the name given to the story of Jesus's birth

patron saint – saint who looks after a particular country or a particular group of people, such as children

pbuh – these letters stand for 'peace be upon him'. Muslims add these words after Muhammad's name and the names of the other prophets.

pilgrimage – special journey made to a holy place

prophet – person chosen by God to be his messenger

recite – say a poem out loud and often learnt off by heart

River Ganges – a river in India, which for Hindus is very holy

saint – person who has lived a very holy life

Shiva – one of the three most important Hindu gods. Shiva is the destroyer of evil in the world.

Shrove – being forgiven for your wrongs, or sins

Sikh – person who follows the Sikh religion, which began in India about 500 years ago

spirit – a being such as a ghost or fairy

tartan – a patterned material made of wool and worn in Scotland

Wise Men – three kings or wise men who came to visit baby Jesus. They brought gifts of gold, frankincense and myrrh.

Index

Advent 12
Allah 8, 9, 10, 11, 30
Angel Jibril 10, 30
baptism 18, 30
Bethlehem 13, 30
Bible 13, 14
Boxing Day 15
carols 14, 30
Chinese New Year 28, 29
Christians 12, 13, 14, 18, 26, 30
Christmas 12–15, 18
churches 12, 14, 30
Epiphany 18
fasting 8, 9, 11, 25, 30
Father Christmas 15
Five Pillars of Islam 9, 11
food 5, 8, 9, 14, 18, 19, 25, 28
Ganesha 24
God 6, 13, 14, 26
Gurdwaras 19, 30
Gurpurbs 19, 30
Guru Gobind Singh 19, 30
Guru Granth Sahib 19
Gurus 19, 30
Hajj 9, 30
Hanukkah 6, 7
Himalayas 24, 30
Hindus 24, 25, 30
Hogmanay 16
hymn 19
Id 11
Id-ul-Fitr 11
Islam 9, 11
Jerusalem 6, 30
Jesus 12, 13, 14, 18, 26, 30

Jews 6, 30
Khalsa 19, 31
lanterns 28
Laylat-ul-Qadr 10
Lent 26
Mahashivrati 24
Makkah 9, 31
mandirs 25, 31
Mary 13
menorah 6, 7, 31
millennium 17
miracles 6, 18, 31
Moon months 5
mosques 11, 31
Muslims 8, 9, 10, 11, 31
nativity play 13, 31
New Year 4, 16–17, 28–29
Parvati 24
patron saints 15, 31
pilgrimages 9, 31
prayers 9, 10, 11, 14, 25
Prophet Muhammad (pbuh) 9, 10, 31
Ramadan 8, 9, 10, 11
River Ganges 25, 31
saints 22, 31
St Valentine's Day 22, 23
Santa Claus 15
Scotland 16, 20
Shiva 24, 25, 31
Shrove Tuesday 26, 31
Sikhs 19, 31
Wise Men 13, 18, 31